Jawaher Al Dossari holds a Master's degree in International Business from University of Wollongong in Dubai. She developed an interest in corporate social responsibility (CSR) when studying her masters, and during her first experience in the field of CSR. Jawaher has extensive experience in CSR from different perspectives; business, government and NGOs. She has a large focus on strategic partnership-building, especially on inter-sector collaborations among different organizations and across various sectors. Jawaher assisted a couple of organizations to take part in large international agencies such as, UNHCR, UNICEF and the UN Global Compact. She is also experienced in Corporate Social Responsibility (CSR) reporting where she developed a number of reports during her work experience in accordance to GRI reporting principles. Jawaher also has extensive experience in CSR policy development, CSR strategy development for organizations and NGOs and also in CSR program development and management.

Jawaher first worked as a manager for Program Development at the Centre for Responsible Business, an initiative by Dubai Chamber to promote the principles of CSR and Business Ethics across the business sector in the UAE. This experience has enriched her skills in the field of CSR and qualified her to join the CSR team at Sama Dubai; one of the subsidiaries owned by Dubai Holding, where she gained a lot of knowledge and experience in CSR from a business perspective. She then moved to Mohammed bin Rashid Al Maktoum Foundation where she managed a couple of programs and initiatives related to human capital development. Jawaher had overseen the foundation's scholarship programs that were offered on a local, regional and international scale. She also managed the Strategy and Business Excellence Office.

Jawaher also worked at the Dubai Foundation for Women and Children, where her main responsibilities fall within the area of acquiring and developing strategic and sustainable partnerships with various organizations from different sectors across the local, regional, and international context. She was also responsible for securing and generating sustainable resources to the foundation. Jawaher held several roles in the foundation such as, Board Executive Committee Member & Secretariat for Legal Affairs, Member of the Projects Committee and Chair of Legislative Committee, where she utilized her skills and expertise in philanthropic foundations set-up and charity governance to set the best governance standards for the foundation. She is now working at the UAE Federal National Council, the Parliament body in the country, in the Parliamentary Communications Sector, the vital arm of the Council that contributes to the country's foreign policy through Parliamentary Diplomacy and dialogue.

Jawaher currently commencing her higher studies Doctor of Philosophy in Business Management at The British University in Dubai. Her studies will be in area of CSR.

For the ones who loved me with honesty
and brought joy to my life.

I dedicate my words,
my heart…
with all its love…
to you…

Sincerely,
Jawaher

Jawaher Al Dossari

UNFINISHED: LOVE

AUSTIN MACAULEY PUBLISHERS™
LONDON • CAMBRIDGE • NEW YORK • SHARJAH

ISBN – 9789948795261 – (Paperback)
ISBN – 9789948795278 – (E-Book)

Application Number: MC-10-01-7192366
Age Classification: E

First Published 2023
AUSTIN MACAULEY PUBLISHERS FZE
Sharjah Publishing City
P O Box [519201]
Sharjah, UAE
www.austinmacauley.ae
+971 655 95 202

I used to seek love, compassion, care, and unconditional
support from others,
till I realized, no one will last forever in my life.

Some stay for a day, weeks, months, and probably few years.
No one can give me all what I want.

It's only me who can become the Giver of:
love,
hope,
care,
support,
and happiness
to myself.

It's all about:
self-love,
self-care,
emotional-independency,
my own happiness,
and self-development…

These are all, from now on, my priority…
I own them,
I control them…

It's ok to be weak,
but with strong love to yourself!

Love yourself first!
you will feel lighter!
your days will get brighter!
You will see happiness then and onwards!

Affirmation of Love

Am with you
Am with you
Am with you
Am with you
Am with you

Anywhere
Everywhere
Every spot
Every second
Every moment

Am with you
Cause I Love You
And cause we belong together

****

When Love Comes Along

And when it came along…
I saw beauty in my life…
I felt peace and happiness…
This love "Your Love" will remain ~ eternally.

****

When Love Becomes Your Home

You are my home…
You are the peace that came into my soul…
You are the one who brought happiness to my life…
You are the *one* who I chose among all …
I love you.

****

When Love Touches Your Bones

My bones,
and my entire nervous system,
this is where does your Love exist,
and comes out from…

****

There Is Still More of Love

I Love You…
I Love the one who I thought of, and
I Love the one who I picked…
I Love You…
This is not enough; and
There's more!

****

A Request

Stay with me ..
Cause I only want you ...

****

Visioning You

I Saw Home… in/with you ♥

****

Why Are You Still Waiting?

Cause destiny is holding me "for you"

****

Heaven

You're my Heaven.
Swiss follows…

****

Only You

I love you all… everything, everything in you…
I love how smart you are… I *melt* for it…
I love your mindset… it makes me believe that you're my
2nd half…
I love the way how you talk… it makes me fall into you
I love the way how you care about me… it makes me love
you more and more
I love your feelings… your love… your words… your
voice… only you…

****

A Wish

With you… a tiny cottage is enough than the world…

****

Remember This!

When you'll visit London city,
someone will whisper my name in your ears…
When you'll spend fall/ autumn season in London,
sit on the chairs of Hyde Park, listen to the trees' movement,
see the lakes and smell the falling leaves,
the images of me and you together will appear in your
mind's eye…
When you'll visit Swiss,
you'll see me "only"…
One day: you'll cry for all of the above… and won't forget
my words…

****

Life Limits

My life starts and ends with you

****

Feeling You

You are not here,
But,
I feel you are everywhere.

****

Endless Love

No withdrawal from you at all… "Eternity" is you.

****

When Happiness Is You

Happiness comes first… You're first…

****

Here…

You're with me… wherever I go…

****

Another Wish

The best is yet to come…
all with you,
beside me.

****

Falling into You

I Fall for Your Words
I Fall for Your Beauty
I Fall for Your Soul
I Fall for Your All…

****

My Light

You're the oxygen that surrounds me… and gets into my
body
You're the breath that fuels life into me…
You're always there… in every blink I see your face…
You're my day and night… every moment in between…
You're my light… you're my shade… and my moon in the
darkness…
You're my family… my friend and the only one…
You're the World…

****

Hidden Message

You…
London…
The weather…
Heaven!

****

Prayers

You are my desire
And being with you is on my daily prayers

****

Won't Let Go

I will hold on to you with all my strength
cause you're the only one who awakened my senses

****

Choices

I choose you again and again and again… etc.

****

Your Gifts

You…
My joy,
My happiness,
My butterflies,
My flame and sparks.

You…
My rebirth,

Again and again.

You…
My air,
My spring,
My sun,
And hope.
You…
My beginnings and endings,
My everyday,
My eternal love,
I Love you…
And it's so deep…
And it's not enough…
And it's not ending…
It's all for you…
Am all for you ....

****

Lasting Forever

I am yours forever… and not a day thing…
My love doesn't vanish… it lasts… it remains… never
ends…
cause you exist in me…
I breathe you…
My love will last till the last breath…

****

My Destiny

You're my Home…
In your hands I feel whole…
With you I tasted love…
I touched the sky…
And I reached Heaven…
Your love is my home…
You're my home…
My Destiny…
I am enough with you…

****

It Keeps Renewing

As a circle,
my love for you,
starts and ends,
from one point to the same…
and I will love you always,
as if I just fallen in you,
and continue loving you forever ♥

****

When Life Starts with You Every Day

You cannot imagine how much I miss hearing your voice…
"You bring life to me"…
At the beginning of everyday,
And peace at the end of each day…
I love you …

****

Confirmation

My love for you is unstoppable!
my love for you is a certainty.

****

When You Are Able to See Through

Liars… betrayers… can be seen…
Only honest people, can see their fake stories…

****

Unfair Treatment

She was faithful and honest,
Her love was innocent,
She deserved no more than a kind and gentle heart…

****

Pain Has an End

She's in pain… but life goes on…
She will pass this phase and survive…
Happy endings will come once faith is in heart…
Her soul deserves happiness, and God will hand it over…

****

Love Needs a Man

Move on my dear,
He is not worth it…
Cause your love
Needs someone;
Brave,
Gentle,
And sincere.

****

She Is Far Away from His Darkness

He couldn't handle honesty
He couldn't handle my light
He wanted to be under the shade
And drag me right there!
Am way above

Am like a sun

****

Follow the Light

Your intuition is your light!
It is right!
Truth shines…
And lighten your path…

****

Healing Is a Process

He left my heart cracked
He burned my soul
Am in flames
Waiting for my ashes to blow in the wind
To heal
And rebirth

****

Gratitude

Gratitude will heal you
Will protect you
Practice it,
Feel it, and

Breathe it.

****

You'll Rise Again

It's ok
Time passes
You'll rise
You'll shine

****

When Truth Hurts

My Gut tells me everything I need to know
I hate it…
Cause I feel it in my bones!

****

Feeling Weak for a Day

My heart is heavy
And wounded…
My soul is in flames
My body is burning…
I feel strangled…
I lost my strength
I choke with every breath

I want to live
I want to rise
I have to survive
I need to heal myself
I deserve a new chance
A better life…

****

Waking Me up Again

It broke me
But
It fixed my vision

****

A Truth

Unfinished relationships
Unhealed ♡ 🔥

****

It's Only for a While

It wasn't over for me
I waited for you…
I couldn't move on
You numbed me…

Am stuck…

****

Grateful

I was praying to God not to lose you
And I lost you
It's God decision
That's God destiny
It's the best for me
And am grateful

****

Stay Strong

Hold on
Don't you dare get tired
And fall…
You'll rise
You'll shine
You'll spark

****

What a Fool

He handed me the scissors
To cut him-off

****

Even Your Absence Is Heaven!

You're the love that came to my life without warning
And left in silence
You're a pain with no healing
We are unfinished
And there's no undo to us
I am in love with you – but
Your absence is heaven

****

You're Burned

You're dead
I'll bury your love
I see no you
You're burned
Your ashes are gone
Along with the wind…

****

God's Grace

God's grace surrounds me
Don't you ever think I won't pass you
I'll step on you soon
The more I love you, the more I hate having you in my life
Don't underestimate my power
It is as much as my love to you…
So weigh it…

****

Remember This Too

You'll remember my love
You'll hear my voice
You'll see me in every corner in your room
You'll feel me alive in your home
You'll see me in your mom
Each hour, has it's own memory of us
Remember us?
You won't forget us
You won't forget me
You won't pass me
You'll come back again
Seeking forgiveness
Cause everybody comes back to me
And I do not!

****

How Much He Worths

I cannot resist this love
My memories are all about you
I love you as much as I hate you
You do not deserve this all
You do not deserve me
I am a *gem*
And you are not even worth "sand"

****

You'll Live as Miserable as Your Love

You'll feel lonely
You'll feel empty
You'll be unloved
You'll search for me
Begging for my love
To keep you alive…
I love you so much… but,
It'll be too late…

****

Pain Will Continue with You

Our story is unfinished
no return
not even in dreams, shall we ever meet

"hope" has turned to ashes
no more love
pain will remain unhealed
The suffer may end,
But

memories won't leave
You won't let go

****

Am Protected

There's no more chaos
My heart is in peace
Am safe now
But
There's a corner
Where pain is locked in

****

A Weak Moment

There's so much of you in me,
cannot pull you out of my ribs.

****

Locating Memories

Memories are engraved in our hearts
Who said in minds!
That's why they don't go away!
****

Home Sick

Once upon a time
You were my home
You took the peace from it
You stole the life
And left only the storms
Am home sick
Wanting you and our home

****

Old Story

The real love story is you…
only you…
you walked with me all along
till you left my hands…
you couldn't handle true love
It's far away from your lower standards

****

You will Be Shocked

Do not underestimate my power
or my strength
it is equal to my love
that used to be
I can handle it
I can leave you easily
you'll suffer the loss

****

Our Choices

We have no choices in whom to love
But we can choose to leave when love is not even!
Save your heart!
Save your love for one who's worth
Reserve this treasure you have for the right one!
****

Believe Me

This scar you caused
I'll be forever proud if it
As I won my life back
My mind is freed
My hands are unchained
But
My heart is tied to yours

* * * * * * * * * * * *

Another Moment of Weakness

I am not sad
My sorrows will vanish soon
I just miss the fake you

* * * * * * * * * * * *

A Message

To whom it may concern
To the one and only
I love you
But
I do not want you
Ever…

* * * * * * * * * * * *

Beauty and the Beast

Her soul was a complete beauty
While the beast was hidden in yours

* * * * * * * * * * * *

Your Regrets

You will go away with the crowd
You'll think you have a better life
By time
You won't sleep every night
You'll remember my worth
You'll keep
Whispering and repeating words of regrets
Till you fall asleep
You'll wake up realizing how much you need me
Remembering the day you lost me
Regretting every moment without me
And, I'll be fine without you!

****

I Am Living

Am alive,
Breathing.
I don't need you!

****

You Will Feel the Pain

I love you as much as your sins
As much as the disappointment you've caused
You'll realize this very late…

You'll be left behind, living in sorrow and regret
You'll beg for my love

****

God's Love

There's something good behind our breakup
God's gift
God's love
And protection
For His Jewels
And not your evil

****

Unfortunate Feelings

I felt balanced with you
I lived Peace with you
The more the love I have for you
The more is the pain that I feel
The more the sorrow
The more the choking I get used to
Without you and with your pains
I Love You, unfortunately!

****

When It Is Unfinished, It Is Eternal

I am escaping from you,
To you.
I am not sure if I'll be able to get over you!

We are an unfinished story,
We are "eternal".

****

Another Moment of Weakness

They say:
Time toughens
Time forgets
Time heals
Will I be able?
My love has no validity
I am stuck in a life of yours in
I paused there
My love won't cease 💔

****

Those Days When Am Weak

Always remember
When am in those sad days
Feeling down

Broken
Laying with my sorrows only
Those days are when I Love You the most

****

Our Clock

7:15 am good morning my love
3:15 pm I Love You
5:15 pm I Love You
9:15 pm I still Love You
12:15 am good night my one & only…
It's 7:15 am again, and I still love you…
The clock keeps running
In circle…
Same as my love
Nothing changed…
It won't end
It is permanent
You're in my whole day,
Hours and seconds
Each tick, calls for you
And says "I Miss You badly"

****

Born Again

Born again
Not slave to your love
Not even in your dreams I am
You are dead to me
Since the day you left quietly
I knew you're not coming back
So I buried your story
The unfinished one!
Your fabricated feelings
Your lies
And your fake love words
Am Born again…
Breathing easily…

****

When Apologies Get Confused

I can't apologize for the pain he caused to me
I can't apologize for him leaving me behind for no reason
Except that he can't be loyal
I apologize for myself, for believing his lies

****

I Won't Be Nice to You

I am a nice woman
But… you've revealed the beast in me
And you'll never see me nice to you anymore…

****

Definition of Love

Real love is nothing more than
feeling safe…
being understood, and
respected…
If you find it, grab it…

****

Move Towards the Light

I had to burn all the bridges
So, there's no ever returns
No return to stress…
Anxiety…
Doubts.
Sometimes, it's a relief
To never look back
Just move forward towards the light 💡

****

I Changed

I am no longer the same person you knew two years ago
In fact,
Am not that person who was yesterday
Every day, a page from my life flips
I flipped you as well
I have washed my hands of you
I am no longer the same person who needs you
Loves you
Breathe you
I am alive by myself
I am full of self-love
I do not need you… Honestly…

****

Another Wish

I just have one wish
Before you leave…
Please shut the door, and
Never think of turning back…
You're *unwanted!*
Not anymore…

****

I Took the Risk

I knew it won't last long
hell, it didn't
and I continued anyway…
till it tore me apart…

****

Leaving in Silence

Leaving in silence
with unfinished conversations
un-ended relation
is so damn painful
and unforgettable!

****

Scars Exist

My scars are from the loved ones
Never are from my enemies…
That's a lesson I never learned
Till now 💔

****

Another Truth and Advice

Your doubts
Are signs…
Your thoughts
Are all facts
And real…
Yes, you are right…
Trust your *gut*!

****

Loving Yourself

Love yourself, girl.
You deserve your own love.
It will give you strength.
It shall fill you with power.
Stop searching for others to love you!

****

When You Left

Whatever thing you pushed me away from,
I achieved it when you left.
I succeeded, with high distinction!

****

Advice

Silence is self-respect,
especially with liars and betrayers…
Protect your mental health,
and keep your standards *up*!

****

A Message to Rise-Up

No regrets, for betrayers,
Liars.
No grieving, for untrue love,
Dishonesty.
Rise-up…
Your heart's worth a real man.
Stand-up…
Your life deserves happiness…

****

Another Moment of Weakness

I broke my heart many times,
For people who do not love me,
And I love them so deep.
How miserable I am?
My heart falls for the wrong ones.
For the ones whom do not love me!

****

A Message to a Friend

Don't expose yourself.
You'll always be valuable to them…

****

Another Truth

You will only realize how much they loved you,
When they leave…
Remember that!

****

A Note to a Friend

They will remember you when they are with another
partner…
They will realize then,
That they will never win you back again…
Trust me my friend…
They will miss you badly once they start comparing the new
one with the old you…
Trust me, and
Trust Karma…
They will cry for you… once they hear your name called
anywhere…
They will feel your pain.

They will be ashamed for their betrayals.
You won't be forgotten…
They will suffer at the end…

****

Lessons of Life

Never feel guilty for loving the wrong one.
It is an experience.
You will learn.
You will be strong.
You will be smart.
Remember!

****

I Pity You

I was blind.
I couldn't see the emptiness in your eyes,
The darkness in your soul.
You are Evil!
I pity you…

****

Peace

Never seek for closure with dishonest ones.
God gave you Peace!
It's a Gift…

****

Love Yourself Deeply

Get up and rise!
You need to feel spring in an autumn day.
You better get over it, and
Close this chapter,
Erase this story.
Trust your power!
And love yourself…
Become your self-lover.
Be emotionally independent.

****

Weak Moments

Am screaming in silence.
Can you hear me?
No, you can't…
Cause, you've never heard my voice when I was calling for
you…
You're selfish.

****

No Regrets

My turn-back moment was when I gave up on you…
It hurt me…
I knew there's no coming back again…
And I moved the steering in the nearest turn…
No regrets!
Good bye…

****

You'll be Confused

I will give you chances.
But, you will never know which is the last one…

****

You Opened My Eyes

I didn't know how toxic you were,
Till you pushed me towards the light…
I realized what a person you are!
So awful!

****

Another Moment of Weakness

What a loser I am!
Nobody loved me the way I did.
I failed myself,
I failed cause am honest!

****

Your Evil Is Weak

My love was so deep, as you couldn't handle.
The darkness in you,
The fake,
The evil,
Could not face me…
I am supported by God!

****

Another Moment of Weakness

My tears,
Are heavy,
Burning,
Cannot handle a drop on my cheek…
They're stuck,
Am in pain.

****

Remember This Too

My patience with you is measured by time.
Like an hourglass…
Count the sands…
Till the last grain of sand…
My patience ends here,
And the glass cannot be flipped…
It only breaks…
And cannot be fixed…
Imagine this and keep it in your mind!

****

Your Intuitions Are Not Illusions

When you see the signs,
Trust them!
Never doubt your intuitions!
Believe me… they're not illusions…

****

Advice

If you do not feel peace in it,
Then let it go…
Don't waste your energy, and
Don't ruin your mental health!

****

Get Lost!

Shut up!
Get out!
Get lost!
You're full of shit,
You do not deserve a Gem like me!

****

The Power of Woman

I thought…
My heart will not be able to get over you.
In less than a month,
I forgot how you look like!

****

Gone for Good

Gone for good
for the good of my life
for my happiness…
for my peace
Gone for good…
So grateful for God's destiny!

****

Good Memories Also Disappear

Sometimes I think of you at midnight,
And sometimes early morning…
But, you know what,
I have no feelings for you,
I never miss you with every single thought!
Your messes destroyed all our good memories!
This is what you created…
And am so glad for that…
It Helped me get over you easily!

****

You Are Unforgiven

The pain you caused.
The anxiety you brought.
The mess you left…
The sorrow you created…
Are all deep…
Down into the bones!
That's why, you will not be forgiven!

****

When Your Soul Needs to Be Light

I will never forgive you,
Cause you do not exist…
But, I will forgive myself,
For loving someone like you…
I need to free my soul…

****

It's Only a Dream

We dreamt together
Walked around the lanes of London
We flew to Swiss together
Used to be our heaven
We loved Paris
Our relation started with a conversation about the city of
love
We dreamt of many cities
Altogether…
We settled in Colorado
Our dream home
But, at the end
We had two different final destinations
We are far away from each other
Our dreams never came true!

****

A Confession

Whenever you come into my mind
I feel disgusted
Disappointed
Ashamed
For loving someone like you
For wasting my time… words…
And my thoughts on you…

****

I Healed Myself

I saw a therapist
After our silent breakup.
She couldn't manage to heal me!
In fact,
I healed myself.
I woke up my inner power.
I recovered very soon.
Girl…
You do not need a friend or a therapist
To help you get over your bad chapters of life…
You are the therapist of your own.
You are your friend.
You can kill the victim in you
And stand-up alone.

Love yourself!
Heal yourself!
You *can*!

****

Blooming Without You

I bloomed when you left…

****

No More You

I see no more you
I hear not your voice
No more senses of you
You are forgotten…
That is God's Gift…
I am blessed…

****

Unfinished Stories

Unfinished stories
Are the worst,
The most painful…

Just like a sudden death of a loved one!

****

The Day Will Come

One day,
they will regret;
every action of disappointment
every hurt
every lie
they will regret failing you…
so, be ready for that day!

****

God's Mercy

We are not alone.
God is always there to protect us.
We have all the choices,
But, God decides our fate.
His decision is always the right one,
And best for us!
Believe in God 🙏
Trust the path he plans for you…

****

Respect Comes First

Sweet words
Nice actions

Will never be equal to respect!
All are disregarded if respect is not there!

****

You Were Rejected

I inhaled your Love
But, my body rejected it…
Your love was toxic!

****

No Doors for You

I opened the door,
Cleared the path,
For you to walk away…
Do not come back!
I changed the locks!

****

Another Advice

Nobody can pull you down.
You can grow.
You will rise.
You shall glow.

****

A Tough Goodbye

Our goodbye was so quiet,
Tearless,
But full of pain…
It's one of the hardest goodbyes 💔

****

Only When Am Weak

Yes, I miss you,
Only when am weak…
Only when am powerless…
Yes, I miss you,
Badly…
I Love You…
Endlessly…

****

One of a Kind

You were one of a kind.
A fake one!
I realized it too late…
After falling into you…

****

Unforgettable Dreams

Our favorite city
will always be London
Our best season
will always be autumn
Our special moments
will always be around the falling leaves of autumn
Our secret spot
will always be the benches of Holland Park
Our walking time
will always be after lunch
London
autumn
leaves
benches
lunch
None can be forgotten!

****

A Note to the One

You are the one
I knew it from day one
Your love…
You…
Leaving me…
Alone in silence…
Un-ended love…
Undone with you…
This all,
Gave me the courage to write…
Pushed me strongly to note down my feelings…
You made me embroider my feelings into words…
You created an Author
A Poet!
Thank you for that!
And thank you for leaving me!
I became who I am now…
Full of strength and power…
Lots of Love!

****

Death vs Betrayal

With loss of trust,
There are no more memories.
All are ruined and buried with your story!
As it is said:

"Losing someone for death is much easier to handle than
losing trust."
Sometimes I wonder, what is much easier to handle?
I guess "Betrayal" kills everything!

****

Falls Followed by Rises

I never regretted quitting my job.
Lots of doors opened that I couldn't imagine.
It was a tough decision!
It took me a year to handle unemployment.
I managed to create my new path;
self-relief,
happiness,
independency,
self-development.
Yes… it was a right decision!

****

Be Careful

There is
no more welcoming
for liars
betrayers
no more forgiving…
Be careful!

As it is said:
"The dog's tail will never straighten out"
Save yourself once and not twice from the same
circumstance!

****

A Message for a Friend

Girl…
Fall in love with whatever you love.
Enjoy the feeling…
But,
If it harms you,
Learn how to quit
In the exact timing!
Girl…
Don't fall forever,
Cause nothing lasts!

****

When Day One Becomes the Last

He said I Love You,
on day one!
My heart couldn't stop beating.
I was unhappy,
worried,
anxious,

tensed!
During the entire journey,
I had that bad feeling!
I knew it from day one.
This Love,
he's confessing,
will not last!
And it did not!
I saw the ending from day one!

****

Strays Are Unwelcomed

There is no room for you anymore.
You are unwanted,
Unwelcomed…
I am not a shelter,
For strays.
I have no roof,
To protect you!
I have no love,
To feed you!
My home is the clouds.
I live there,
Like an angel.
Protected by God!
You will always be down there,
lost,
straying,
for love,

care,
and for guidance…
Enjoy your miserable life!
You deserve it!

****

Angel vs Evil

Our mindsets connected.
Our intellectual conversations never ended.
Our hearts were melting for each other.
While,
Our souls were opposites!
Never matched,
Cause Evil and Angel do not blend…
Ever!
****

Another Advice

I cannot tolerate fake people.
I reached the point,
Where my mental health comes first…
So, my advice:
Delink yourself from all fake people,
You will live longer!

****

Life Experiences Are Learning Paths

Twilight your soul!
Get rid of this trauma.
You are not a victim.
You are in a learning experience.
You'll get over it soon.

****

Another Advice

You come first!
Your family comes next…
After that;
It is all *you*…
Nothing else!

****

When Silence Is a Punishment

I do not need to punish you.
My silence is enough!
All our memories,
Shall be your greater punishment!
You'll be haunted with our memories…

****

Another Moment of Weakness

I haven't deleted our conversations yet!
I haven't removed you from my social media accounts till
now!
Am Waiting,
For a message.
Am Expecting,
A greeting for Eid,
At least, or
My birthday!
The Eid occasions passed, and
Nothing came yet from you.
Still waiting to hear from you on
August 29.
Then, I'll decide what to do!

****

Confusion

I am not sure am waiting for what?
A new chapter with you!
A new beginning!
Or,
A *closure*!
It's very hard!

****

Your Loss!

I sympathize with you!
You cannot win me back.
You cannot bring back my love into your life
You failed loving me!
You lack honesty!
My deepest condolences, and
Sorry for your loss!

****

You Are a Fraud

I sensed your betrayal from the day you started cheating.
I knew it!
You are a *fraud*!
I smelled it,
It stinks.
I saw it,
It disgusts.
I never spoke about it!
I swallowed the sorrows till I choked…
I was weak that time…
Unconscious…
Blind…
Deaf…
Speechless!
But, I was blessed by God's Mercy…
He rescued me!

I survived… as a result of His Love!

****

Don't Come Back in My Thoughts Again!

When I think of you,
I feel numbed,
As if I am losing myself,
My senses, and
My soul!
My body is rejecting you,
As my mind does!
So, please do not come back even in my thoughts!
Am alive without you!

****

Stop Acting as the Victim

You did not bother to call
Or text…
Then,
Why are you upset with me?
You walked away,
And I shut the door after you!
I changed the locks too,
And buried the keys!
It was very simple for you,
And was easily handled by me!

So, stop living in a trauma you created!
Stop Acting as the *victim*!

****

You Set Me Free Easily

I was trapped in a bubble,
Filled out with toxic air.
It was your love…
I was stuck there…
Praying to be released one day…
I didn't have the courage or strength to leave.
I feared losing you…
My heart became heavy,
Carrying the sorrows,
Of your lies.
My eyes were filled,
With burning tears.
You pushed me away suddenly,
It was a simple step from your side!
You tore this love,
And set me free…

****

Classy Love by a Fraud

Our love…
was right,
unique,
distinguished,
very classy,
but, you were a *fraud*!

****

A Note to You… Fraud

If I miss you,
It means
Am in a bad mood,
Or
In my worst moments!
As if you may know:
Negative thoughts always come with negative feelings!
Remember that!

****

CPSIA information can be obtained
at www.ICGtesting.com
Printed in the USA
BVHW051137060623
665472BV00014B/1371